CW00553537

Share
Our
Wealth

Share
Our
Wealth

A Manual for the Share
Our Wealth Society

HUEY P. LONG

NEW YORK

Share Our Wealth: A Manual for the Share Our Wealth Society.
Originally published in 1934.
This edition published by Cosimo Classics in 2020.

Cover copyright © 2020 by Cosimo, Inc.
Cover image, photo of Senator Huey Long leaving the Senate floor after a
five-and-half-hour fillibuster during the 74th Congress, August 27, 1935.
Harris & Ewing Collection, Library of Congress. Image sourced from
Wikimedia Commons, *https://commons.wikimedia.org/wiki/File:Huey_
Long_1935_LOC_hec_39385.jpg*

Cover design by www.heatherkern.com.

ISBN: 9781646797592

This edition is a replica of a rare classic. As such, it is possible that some
of the text might be blurred or of reduced print quality. Thank you for
your understanding, and we wish you a pleasant reading experience.

Cosimo aims to publish books that inspire, inform, and engage readers worldwide. We use innovative print-on-demand technology that
enables books to be printed based on specific customer needs. This
approach eliminates an artificial scarcity of publications and allows us
to distribute books in the most efficient and environmentally sustainable manner. Cosimo also works with printers and paper manufactur-
ers who practice and encourage sustainable forest management, using
paper that has been certified by the FSC, SFI, and PEFC whenever
possible.

Ordering Information:
Cosimo publications are available at online bookstores. They may also be
purchased for educational, business, or promotional use:
Bulk orders: Special discounts are available on bulk orders for reading
groups, organizations, businesses, and others.
Custom-label orders: We offer selected books with your customized cover
or logo of choice.

For more information, contact us at www.cosimobooks.com.

EDUCATIONAL PROGRAM
FOR SHARE OUR WEALTH SOCIETY

Government Assumes the Cost and Burden to Guarantee College, Professional, and Vocational Education to All Students

Under the present policy of government the young man and young woman whose parents are possessed of means can be given a college education or vocational and professional training. There are some exceptions to this rule; that is to say, that in some few cases students can find work by which to pay their expenses through college. As a general rule, however, only those with parents possessing extraordinary means can attend college.

"All men are created equal," says the Declaration of Independence, and to all those born the Constitution of our Nation guarantees "life, liberty, and the pursuit of happiness."

These provisions of our immortal national documents are not observed when the right to education rests upon the financial ability of one's parents rather than upon the mental capacity of a student to learn and his energy to apply himself to the proper study necessary for him to learn.

The "share our wealth" program contemplates that from the billions of excess revenue brought into the United States Treasury by limiting fortunes to a few million dollars to any one person, that such large sums will be expended by the Government as will afford college education and professional training to all students based upon their mental capacity and energy rather than upon the wealth of their parents. Such an education contemplates not only the scholarship but such supplies and living costs as a student may have in order to attend college.

This will transfer the youth of our land into making preparation for building a better and greater nation. It will take their surplus labor out of the ranks of employment and afford more room for others; it will mean an immediate expansion of our educational facilities and the bringing back into active service of hundreds of thousands of learned instructors whose intellect and capacities, now idle, may be used for the moral, spiritual, and intellectual uplift of the Nation. Architects, engineers, builders, material men, and craftsmen now idle would find extensive and continued field for employment in providing and maintaining such extended educational facilities in the Nation.

All in all, the program is one of national organization; it means no great or burdensome outlay because there is a surplus of the goods and things needed for the care of all students, and the consuming of the same will immediately aid our problems of over-production.

HUEY P. LONG,
United States Senator.

PRINCIPLES AND PLATFORM:

1. To limit poverty by providing that every deserving family shall share in the wealth of America for not less than one-third of the average wealth, thereby to possess not less than $5,000 free of debt.

2. To limit fortunes to such a few million dollars as will allow the balance of the American people to share in the wealth and profits of the land.

3. Old Age Pensions of $30 per month to persons over 60 years of age who do not earn as much as $1,000 per year or who possess less than $10,000 in cash or property, thereby to remove from the field of labor, in times of unemployment, those who have contributed their share to the public service.

4. To limit the hours of work to such an extent as to prevent over-production and to give the workers of America some share in the recreations, conveniences and luxuries of life.

5. To balance agricultural production with what can be sold and consumed according to the laws of God, which have never failed.

6. To care for the Veterans of our wars.

7. Taxation to run the government to be supported, first, by reducing big fortunes from the top, thereby to improve the country and provide employment in public works whenever agricultural surplus is such as to render unnecessary, in whole or in part, any particular crop.

"Go ye into all communities and preach the
Gospel to every living creature."

MANUAL

SUGGESTED FOR

SHARE OUR WEALTH SOCIETY

"EVERY MAN A KING"

REGULAR MEETINGS

Each Society, however large or small, should arrange to have regular meetings. This may be once each week, or once each month. As often as possible, the meetings should be open to the public so that the purposes for the society may be made known to everybody and the membership thereby increased. The day and hour for meetings should be decided in accordance with what is best in each community. In some places this time might best be some evening, or night, of the week. In other places a Saturday or Sunday afternoon might be the best time to meet.

SPECIAL MEETINGS AND PROGRAMS

Whenever the membership may be enlarged and more people may be brought into contact with the aims and purposes of this society, public programs should be arranged at which the needs and purposes for the organization may be explained.

At all meetings articles should be read and, when possible, speeches should be made, showing, 1st: The need for spreading the wealth and work in America; and 2nd: The conditions now existing in America because the wealth is concentrated in the hands of the few, contrary to the laws of God and the purposes of our Declaration of Independence and Constitution of the United States.

That all may know, without question, that we are on the right track and trying to do what is necessary to save our people, there is included in this manual, following the speech I delivered, the quotations from the Laws of Our Lord and the Gospel of Christ, together with the pertinent passages taken from the Declaration of Independence and from the remarks of leading statesmen, philosophers and learned men of all times and climes.

2

At all meetings plans and arrangements should be made for a constant effort to enlist the whole people of the neighborhood or community to join in this movement and undertaking to free all the American people from an economic and financial enslavement because of there being no limit on the luxury of the few and no protection against the poverty and destitution of the masses.

NUMBER OF MEMBERS FOR SOCIETY

It is necessary, first, that each community have a society, or many societies where it serves best to get members. A live membership of ten is better than a sleeping membership of one hundred.

After the society is first organized and put to work, then the next thing to do is to get as many members as possible. Already there have been formed societies in which nearly every person of age in the whole community has enlisted for membership. One community with 5,000 adult inhabitants reports nearly that number of members in their society. Several other societies report almost as successful organization.

All that is necessary to get members is for the people to know what the work is we are undertaking. There is a certain amount of ignorance to be overcome. Newspapers and magazines, owned and controlled by the money masters, have spread so much false propaganda that many people who read the most are the most ignorant and deluded on the cause of conditions now prevailing and the simple manner by which they **could be corrected.**

ORGANIZATION AND MEMBERSHIP COMMITTEES

Each society should, where possible, have two committees as follows:

    1st: A committee in charge of the work of securing members; and

    2nd: A committee to go into other communities and neighborhoods to get societies organized in them.

The work of getting members and stirring other communities to action should not be confined to the members of two committees, however. They should have the help of every member of the Society in their efforts.

QUALIFICATIONS FOR PERSONS WHO SPEAK AT MEETINGS, ORGANIZE SOCIETIES AND SOLICIT MEMBERS

Let us bear in mind that we are organizing to work for all humanity. Let us bear in mind that our chief work is to have the people know the truth. If only our people could but awake tomorrow understanding the facts which concern and control their living and existence, our fight would be won. But even among our most affluent people, their ignorance sometimes becomes even more dense than the men on the bottom with less chance to learn.

So it is first necessary that the members of a society should not look to our so-called "leaders" to do all the work or to make the arguments and debate the facts. There are just as good and useful men and women for this work at the plow handles, in the factories and on the crossties, people who can organize, secure members, and explain our problems in meetings, as there are in law offices and counting houses.

We want men and women who are not only willing to work for their own deliverance, but who will work for the relief and deliverance of humanity, to feel no embarrassment in speaking out in meeting. Where there is honesty and sincerity, the genuine love for humanity in the soul of a man or woman, there is all the capacity required for the work that can save America. One truthful word from that kind of person is worth a thousand meaningless phrases that an orator can utter.

Tell the truth; hear the truth; know the truth.

NO DUES OR ASSESSMENTS

It must be understood that there are no dues or assessments to be made on any member joining a society. Most of the people have not the money to pay dues, and, when there is need for a little sum to defray a little item of expense (which should never be very much) it must come from voluntary contribution. Avoid creating any items of expense. Look about and get a free meeting place; get some members or some friends to do everything free that you can.

A few dollars contributed voluntarily now and then by those who will feel able to do so, will pay all the costs that should be required of a society. Let the men and women understand they are not expected to give anything.

If this society succeeds in its purpose it will save the people from the misery of ourselves and others. It will remove the des-

4

titute and helpless from the paths and byways. Humanity will be fed, clothed and housed with what we have in abundance. Our work is the highest kind of charity, an effort that all should be blessed through what they produce and create. Therefore, a benefit function or entertainment similar to those given in communities for other worthy purposes could well be used to raise the small amount that any society might ever want to expend for any purpose.

Bear in mind that a society can exist and do great work without raising a dime. Just do not spend anything if you have not the money and go on with this work just the same. Nothing could do this movement more harm than to have the matter of raising money constantly injected into it. We must get the countless thousands of human beings on the bottom into this move and show them how to help us fight for their good and our good. Therefore, let no one of them have cause to feel that one cent is expected of him for any purpose. Keep money raising as far away from this society as you can.

PLAN AND PURPOSE

There is in America today more food of all kinds than al the people could eat if they all had everything they wanted to eat

There is in America today more clothing and clothing ma terial than all the people could wear if they all had all they wante to wear.

There are houses already built in America (and plenty o materials to build more houses) that would give everybody th best comforts of home life.

But greed, avarice and selfishness of the money master have seized the control of all these good things. They let th food rot because the hungry cannot buy it; they let the clothe fall to pieces because the naked cannot buy them; they let th walls fall from the inside of the houses because they had rathe have people walking the streets than to have their greed curbed.

So in this land of plenty, the decay of humanity is at han because we have too much.

We have had many promises from men that they wer going to correct this condition. Some of them have tried to d it. Some tried until the going got rough and quit trying any mor More of them tried and were about to succeed when they wer fortunate enough to get so much of this world's goods that i was to their interest to forget about the balance of the peopl

5

We do not propose to say there shall be no rich men. We do not ask to divide the wealth. We only propose that, when one man gets more than he and his children and children's children can spend or use in their lifetimes, that then we shall say that such person has his share. That means that a few million dollars is the limit to what any one man can own.

When we limit how high one can go, we then limit how low one can fall. We say that two-thirds of the average wealth of any family is enough to have for gain or loss in trade or exchange. Therefore, one-third the average wealth per family should be guaranteed to every worthy and deserving American family, which would mean a home and comforts, education and some of the luxuries of life to everyone, the elimination of poverty,—the promise of God to a nation that does not allow its wealth to be concentrated in the hands of the few.

We propose that men should work so long as their toil is needed to produce enough for everybody and no more. The hours of work will be so limited and the work spread so that all may labor their share of the time required for the land to have plenty. But science and machinery would be a boon and not a curse to the race. These inventions would lessen the toil of all, provide more for their luxury, give the ease and leisure needed for life and the chance of education for all.

Old aged pensions would remove from the ranks and by-ways those of mature life who have contributed their share of the country's effort and toil, not as a matter of their being indigents, not as a charity, but in payment by the nation for the life services adequately performed.

Adequate care for those who have fought our wars would be given.

The funds for such program would all come by limiting fortunes to such few millions of dollars as would be sufficient for any person and his children and their children in their lifetimes.

Income, inheritance and capital levy taxes steadily levied every year would prevent the accumulation of any fortune so big as would prevent the food, clothes and other products of the nation from being fairly shared by and distributed among the people. The tax money thus collected would support the work of the government, spread the wealth among all the people, leaving the tax burden to be borne only by those with accumulations beyond their means.

6

In our best times there has been near to an average yearly income of $5,000 to the family—though some families toiling from sun up to sun down received less that $500 for the whole year. Our fault is not the lack of income; it is the lack of its distribution in a fair manner among the people, which has resulted that a few people now own more than all the balance of the 120,000,000 people in America put together. We do not propose to guarantee the same income to everybody, but by limiting big fortunes and the hours of toil we do propose a comfortable living for all, because in a land with too much of everything, why should anyone be denied that of which the nation has an abundance?

"EVERY MAN A KING"

Radio Address by Senator Huey P. Long, of Louisiana,
February 23, 1934

**Is that a right of life when the young children
of this country are being reared into a sphere
which is more owned by 12 men than it is by
120,000,000 people?**

Ladies and Gentlemen:—

I have only 30 minutes in which to speak to you this evening, and I, therefore, will not be able to discuss in detail so much as I can write when I have all of the time and space that is allowed me for the subjects, but I will undertake to sketch them very briefly without manuscript or preparation, so that you can understand them so well as I can tell them to you tonight.

I contend, my friends, that we have no difficult problem to solve in America, and that is the view of nearly everyone with whom I have discussed the matter here in Washington and elsewhere throughout the United States—that we have no very difficult problem to solve.

It is not the difficulty of the problem which we have; it is the fact that the rich people of this country—and by rich people I mean the super-rich—will not allow us to solve the problems, or rather the one little problem that is afflicting this country, because in order to cure all of our woes it is necessary to scale down the big fortunes, that we may scatter the wealth to be shared by all of the people.

We have a marvelous love for this Government of ours; in fact, it is almost a religion, and it is well that it should be,

7

because we have a splendid form of government and we have a splendid set of laws. We have everything here that we need, except that we have neglected the fundamentals upon which the American Government was principally predicated.

How many of you remember the first thing that the Declaration of Independence said? It said: "We hold these truths to be self-evident, that there are certain inalienable rights for the people, and among them are life, liberty, and the pursuit of happiness;" and it said further, "We hold the view that all men are created equal."

Now, what did they mean by that? Did they mean, my friends, to say that all men are created equal and that that meant that any one man was born to inherit $10,000,000,000 and that another child was to be born to inherit nothing?

Did that mean, my friends, that someone would come into this world without having had an opportunity, of course, to have hit one lick of work, should be born with more than it and all of its children and children's children could ever dispose of, but that another one would have to be born into a life of starvation?

That was not the meaning of the Declaration of Independence when it said that all men are created equal or "That we hold that all men are created equal."

Nor was it the meaning of the Declaration of Independence when it said that they held that there were certain rights that were inalienable—the right of life, liberty, and the pursuit of happiness.

Is that right of life, my friends, when the young children of this country are being reared into a sphere which is more owned by 12 men than it by 120,000,000 people?

Is that, my friends, giving them a fair shake of the dice or anything like the inalienable right of life, liberty, and the pursuit of happiness, or anything resembling the fact that all people are created equal; when we have today in America thousands and hundreds of thousands and millions of children on the verge of starvation in a land that is overflowing with too much to eat and too much to wear?

I do not think you will contend that, and I do not think for a moment that they will contend it.

Now let us see if we cannot return this Government to the Declaration of Independence and see if we are going to do anything regarding it. Why should we hesitate or why should we quibble or why should we quarrel with one another to find out what the difficulty is, when we know that the Lord told us what

8

the difficulty is, and Moses wrote it out so a blind man could see it, then Jesus told us all about it, and it was later written in the Book of James, where everyone could read it?

I refer to the Scriptures, now, my friends, and give you what it says not for the purpose of convincing you of the wisdom of myself, not for the purpose, ladies and gentlemen, of convincing you of the fact that I am quoting the Scriptures means that I am to be more believed than someone else; but I quote you the Scripture, or rather refer you to the Scripture, because whatever you see there you may rely upon will never be disproved so long as you or your children or anyone may live; and you may further depend upon the fact that not one historical fact that the Bible has ever contained has ever yet been disproved by any scientific discovery or by reason of anything that has been disclosed to man through his own individual mind or through the wisdom of the Lord which the Lord has allowed him to have.

But the Scripture says, ladies and gentlemen, that no country can survive, or for a country to survive it is necessary that we keep the wealth scattered among the people, that nothing should keep the wealth scattered among the people, that nothing should be held permanently by any one person, and that 50 years seems to be the year of jubilee in which all property would be scattered about and returned to the sources from which it originally came, and every seventh year debt should be remitted.

Those two things the Almighty said to be necessary—I should say He knew to be necessary, or else He would not have so prescribed that the property would be kept among the general run of the people, and that everyone would continue to share in it; so that no one man would get half of it and hand it down to a son, who takes half of what was left, and that son hand it down to another one, who would take half of what was left, until, like a snowball going downhill, all of the snow was off of the ground except what the snowball had.

I believe that was the judgment and the view and the law of the Lord, that we would have to distribute wealth ever so often, in order that there could not be people starving to death in a land of plenty, as there is in America today.

We have in America today more wealth, more goods, more food, more clothing, more houses than we have ever had. We have everything in abundance here.

We have the farm problem, my friends, because we have too much cotton, because we have too much wheat, and have too much corn, and too much potatoes.

9

We have a home loan problem, because we have too many houses, and yet nobody can buy them and live in them.

We have trouble, my friends, in the country, because we have too much money owing, the greatest indebtedness that has ever been given to civilization, where it has been shown that we are incapable of distributing the actual things that are here, because the people have not money enough to supply themselves with them, and because the greed of a few men is such that they think it is necessary that they own everything, and their pleasure consists in the starvation of the masses, and in their possessing things they cannot use, and their children cannot use, but who bask in the splendor of sunlight and wealth, casting darkness and despair and impressing it on everyone else.

"So, therefore," said the Lord in effect, "if you see these things that now have occurred and exist in this and other countries, there must be a constant scattering of wealth in any country if this country is to survive."

"Then," said the Lord, in effect, "every seventh year there shall be a remission of debts; there will be no debts after 7 years." That was the law.

Now, let us take America today. We have in America today, ladies and gentlemen, $272,000,000,000 of debt. Two hundred and seventy-two thousand millions of dollars of debts are owed by the various people of this country today. Why, my friends, that cannot be paid. It is not possible for that kind of debt to be paid.

The entire currency of the United States is only $6,000,000,000. That is all of the money that we have got in America today. All the actual money you have got in all of your banks, all that you have got in the Government Treasury, is $6,000,000,000; and if you took all that money and paid it out today you would still owe $266,000,000,000; and if you took all that money and paid again you would still owe $260,000,000,000; and if you took it, my friends, 20 times and paid it you would still owe $150,000,000,000.

You would have to have 45 times the entire money supply of the United States today to pay the debts of the people of America and then they would just have to start out from scratch, without a dime to go on with.

So, my friends, it is impossible to pay all of these debts, and you might as well find out that it cannot be done. The United States Supreme Court has definitely found out that it could not be done, because, in a Minnesota case, it held that when a State has postponed the evil day of collecting a debt it was a valid and constitutional exercise of legislative power.

10

Now, ladies and gentlemen, if I may proceed to give you some other words that I think you can understand—I am not going to belabor you by quoting tonight—I am going to tell you what the wise men of all ages and all times, down even to the present day, have all said: That you must keep the wealth of the country scattered, and you must limit the amount that any one man can own. You cannot let any man own $300,000,000,000 or $400,000,-000,000. If you do, one man can own all of the wealth that the United States has in it.

Now, my friends, if you were off on an island where there were 100 lunches, you could not let one man eat up the hundred lunches, or take the hundred lunches and not let anybody else eat any of them. If you did, there would not be anything else for the balance of the people to consume.

So, we have in America today, my friends, a condition by which about 10 men dominate the means of activity in at least 85 percent of the activities that you own. They either own directly everything or they have got some kind of mortgage on it, with a very small percentage to be excepted. They own the banks, they own the steel mills, they own the railroads, they own the bonds, they own the mortgages, they own the stores, and they have chained the country from one end to the other until there is not any kind of business that a small, independent man could go into today and make a living, and there is not any kind of business that an independent man can go into and make any money to buy an automobile with; and they have finally and gradually and steadily eliminated everybody from the fields in which there is a living to be made, and still they have got little enough sense to think they ought to be able to get more business out of it anyway.

If you reduce a man to the point where he is starving to death and bleeding and dying, how do you expect that man to get hold of any money to spend with you? It is not possible.

Then, ladies and gentlemen, how do you expect people to live, when the wherewith cannot be had by the people?

In the beginning I quoted from the Scriptures. I hope you will understand that I am not quoting Scripture to you to convince you of my goodness personally, because that is a thing between me and my Maker; that is something as to how I stand with my Maker and as to how you stand with your Maker. That is not concerned with this issue, except and unless there are those of you who would be so good as to pray for the souls of some of us. But the Lord gave His law, and in the Book of James they said so, that the rich should weep and howl for the miseries that had come upon them; and, therefore, it was written that when the rich hold goods they could not use and could not consume, you will inflict punishment on them, and nothing but days of woe ahead of them.

Then we have heard of the great Greek philosopher, Socrates, and the greater Greek philosopher, Plato, and we have read the dialogue between Plato and Socrates, in which one said that great riches brought on great poverty, and would be destructive of a country. Read what they said. Read what Plato said; that you must not let any one man be too poor, and you must not let any one man be too rich; that the same mill that grinds out the extra rich is the mill that will grind out the extra poor, because, in order that the extra rich can become so affluent, they must necesarily take more of what ordinarily would belong to the average man.

It is a very simple process of mathematics that you do not have to study, and that no one is going to discuss with you.

So that was the view of Socrates and Plato. That was the view of the English statesmen. That was the view of American statesmen. That was the view of American statesmen like Daniel Webster, Thomas Jefferson, Abraham Lincoln, William Jennings Bryan, and Theodore Roosevelt, and even as late as Herbert Hoover and Franklin D. Roosevelt.

Both of these men, Mr. Hoover and Mr. Roosevelt, came out and said there had to be a decentralization of wealth, but neither one of them did anything about it. But, nevertheless, they recognized the principle. The fact that neither one of them ever did anything about it is their own problem that I am not undertaking to criticize; but had Mr. Hoover carried out what he says ought to be done, he would be retiring from the President's office, very probably, 3 years from now, instead of 1 year ago; and had Mr. Roosevelt proceeded along the lines that he stated were necessary for the decentralization of wealth, he would have gone, my friends, a long way already, and within a few months he would have probably reached a solution of all of the problems that afflict this country today.

But I wish to warn you now that nothing that has been done up to this date has taken one dime away from these big fortune-holders; they own just as much as they did, and probably a little bit more; they hold just as many of the debts of the common people as they ever held, and probably a little bit more; and unless we, my friends, are going to give the people of this country a fair shake of the dice, by which they will all get something out of the funds of this land, there is not a chance on the topside

12

of this God's eternal earth by which we can rescue this country and rescue the people of this country.

It is necessary to save the government of the country, but is much more necessary to save the people of America. We love this country. We love this Government. It is a religion, I say. It is a kind of religion people have read of when women, in the name of religion, would take their infant babes and throw them into the burning flame, where they would be instantly devoured by the all-consuming fire, in days gone by; and there probably are some people of the world even today, who, in the name of religion, throw their own babes to destruction; but in the name of our good government, people today are seeing their own children hungry, tired, half-naked, lifting their tear-dimmed eyes into the sad faces of their fathers and mothers, who cannot give them food and clothing they both need, and which is necessary to sustain them, and that goes on day after day, and night after night, when day gets into darkness and blackness, knowing those children would arise in the morning without being fed, and probably go to bed at night without being fed.

Yet in the name of our Government, and all alone, those people undertake and strive as hard as they can to keep a good government alive, and how long they can stand that no one knows. If I were in their place tonight, the place where millions are, I hope that I would have what I might say—I cannot give you the word to express the kind of fortitude they have; that is the word —I hope that I might have the fortitude to praise and honor my Government that had allowed me here in this land, where there is too much to eat and too much to wear, to starve in order that a handful of men can have so much more than they can ever eat or they can ever wear.

Now, we have organized a society, and we call it "Share Our Wealth Society," a society with the motto "Every Man a King."

Every man a king, so there would be no such thing as a man or woman who did not have the necessities of life, who would not be dependent upon the whims and caprices and ipsi dixit of the financial barons for a living. What do we propose by this society? We propose to limit the wealth of big men in the country. There is an average of $15,000 in wealth to every family in America. That is right here today.

We do not propose to divide it up equally. We do not propose a division of wealth, but we propose to limit poverty that we will allow to be inflicted upon any man's family. We will not say we are going to try to guarantee any equality, or $15,000 to a family

13

No; but we do say that one third of the average is low enough for any one family to hold, that there should be a guarantee of a family wealth of around $5,000; enough for a home, an automobile, a radio, and the ordinary conveniences, and the opportunity to educate their children; a fair share of the income of this land thereafter to that family so there will be no such thing as merely the select to have those things, and so there will be no such thing as a family living in poverty and distress.

We have to limit fortunes. Our present plan is that we will allow no one man to own more that $50,000,000. We think that with that limit we will be able to carry out the balance of the program. It may be necessary that we limit it to less than $50,000,000. It may be necessary, in working out of the plans that no man's fortune would be more than $10,000,000 or $15,000,000. But be that as it may, it will still be more than any one man, or any one man and his children and their children, will be able to spend in their lifetimes; and it is not necessary or reasonable to have wealth piled up beyond that point where we cannot prevent poverty among the masses.

Another thing we propose is old-age pension of $30 a month for everyone that is 60 years old. Now, we do not give this pension to a man making $1,000 a year, and we do not give it to him if he has $10,000 in property, but outside of that we do.

We will limit hours of work. There is not any necessity of having overproduction. I think all you have got to do, ladies and gentlemen, is just limit the hours of work to such an extent as people will work only so long as it is necessary to produce enough for all of the people to have what they need. Why, ladies and gentlemen, let us say that all of these labor-saving devices reduce hours down to where you do not have to work but 4 hours a day; that is enough for these people, and then praise be the name of the Lord, if it gets that good. Let it be good and not a curse, and then we will have 5 hours a day and 5 days a week, or even less than that, and we might give a man a whole month off during a year, or give him 2 months; and we might do what other countries have seen fit to do, and what I did in Louisiana, by having schools by which adults could go back and learn the things that have been discovered since they went to school.

We will not have any trouble taking care of the agricultural situation. All you have to do is balance your production with your consumption. You simply have to abandon a particular crop that you have too much of, and all you have to do is store the surplus for the next year, and the Government will take it over.

14

When you have good crops in the area in which the crops that have been planted are sufficient for another year, put in your public works in the particular year when you do not need to raise any more, and by that means you get everybody employed. When the Government has enough of any particular crop to take care of all of the people, that will be all that is necessary; and in order to do all of this, our taxation is going to be to take the billion-dollar fortunes and strip them down to frying size, not to exceed $50,000,000, and if it is necessary to come to $10,000,000, we will come to $10,000,000. We have worked the proposition out to guarantee a limit upon property (and no man will own less than one-third the average), and guarantee a reduction of fortunes and a reduction of hours to spread wealth throughout this country. We would care for the old people above 60 and take them away from this thriving industry and give them a chance to enjoy the necessities and live in ease, and thereby lift from the market the labor which would probably create a surplus of commodities.

Those are the things we propose to do. "Every Man a King." Every man to eat when there is something to eat; all to wear something when there is something to wear. That makes us all a sovereign.

You cannot solve these things through these various and sundry alphabetical codes. You can have the N. R. A. and P. W. A. and C. W. A. and the U. U. G. and G. I. N. and any other kind of dad-gummed lettered code. You can wait until doomsday and see 25 more alphabets, but that is not going to solve this proposition. Why hide? Why quibble? You know what the trouble is. The man that says he does not know what the trouble is is just hiding his face to keep from seeing the sunlight.

God told you what the trouble was. The philosophers told you what the trouble was; and when you have a country where one man owns more than 100,000 people, or a million people, and when you have a country where there are four men, as in America, that have got more control over things than all the 120,000,000 people together, you know what the trouble is.

We had these great incomes in this country; but the farmer, who plowed from sunup to sundown, who labored here from sunup to sundown for 6 days a week, wound up at the end of the time with practically nothing.

And we ought to take care of the veterans of the wars in this program. That is a small matter. Suppose it does cost a billion dollars a year—that means that the money will be scattered throughout this country. We ought to pay them a bonus. We can do it. We ought to take care of every single one of the sick and disabled veterans. I do not care whether a man got sick on the battlefield or did not; every man that wore the uniform of this country is entitled to be taken care of, and there is money enough to do it; and we need to spread the wealth of the country, which you did not do in what you call the N. R. A.

If the N. R. A. has done any good, I can put it all in my eye without having it hurt. All I can see that the N. R. A. has done is to put the little man out of business—the little merchant in his store, the little Italian that is running a fruit stand, or the Greek shoe-shining stand, who has to take hold of a code of 275 pages and study it with a spirit level and compass and looking-glass; he has to hire a Philadelphia lawyer to tell him what is in the code; and by the time he learns what the code is, he is in jail or out of business; and they have got a chain code system that has already put him out of business. The N. R. A. is not worth anything, and I said so when they put it through.

Now, my friends, we have got to hit the root with the ax. Centralized power in the hands of a few, with centralized credit in the hands of a few, is the trouble.

Get together in your community tonight or tomorrow and organize one of our Share Our Wealth Societies. If you do not understand it, write me and let me send you the platform; let me give you the proof of it.

This is Huey P. Long talking, United States Senator, Washington, D. C. Write me and let me send you the data on this proposition. Enroll with us. Let us make known to the people what we are going to do. I will send you a button, if I have got enough of them left. We have got a little button that some of our friends designed, with our message around the rim of the button, and in the center "Every Man a King." Many thousands of them are meeting through the United States, and every day we are getting hundreds and hundreds of letters. Share Our Wealth Societies are now being organized, and people have it within their power to relieve themselves from this terrible situation.

Look at what the Mayo brothers announced this week, these greatest scientists of all the world today, who are entitled to have more money than all the Morgans and the Rockefellers, or anyone else, and yet the Mayos turn back their big fortunes to be used for treating the sick, and said they did not want to lay up fortunes in this earth, but wanted to turn them back where they would do some good; but the other big capitalists are not willing to do that, are not willing to do what these men, 10 times more

16

worthy, have already done, and it is going to take a law to requir
them to do it.

Organize your Share Our Wealth Society and get your peo
ple to meet with you, and make known your wishes to your Sen
ators and Representatives in Congress.

Now, my friends, I am going to stop. I thank you for thi
opportunity to talk to you. I am having to talk under the auspice
and by the grace and permission of the National Broadcastin$
System tonight, and they are letting me talk free. If I had th
money, and I wish I had the money, I would like to talk to you
more often on this line, but I have not got it, and I cannot expec
these people to give it to me free except on some rare instance
But, my friends, I hope to have the opportunity to talk with you
and I am writing to you, and I hope that you will get up and
help in the work, because the resolutions and bills are before
Congress, and we hope to have your help in getting together and
organizing your Share Our Wealth Societies.

Now, that I have but a minute left, I want to say that I
suppose my family is listening in on the radio in New Orleans
and I will say to my wife and three children that I am entirely
well and hope to be home before many more days, and I hope
they have listened to my speech tonight, and I wish them and all
of their neighbors and friends everything good that may be had.

I thank you, my friends, for your kind attention, and I hope
you will enroll with us, take care of your own work in the work
of this Government, and share or help in our Share Our Wealth
Societies.

I thank you.

AUTHORITY AND STATISTICS

"Ill fares the land to hastening ills a prey,
Where wealth accumulates and men decay.
Princes and lords may flourish or may fade,
A breath can make them as a breath has made.
But a bold peasantry, their country's pride,
When once destroyed, can never be supplied."

—Goldsmith

FROM THE BIBLE:

"The Lord is our law giver."
—*Isaiah: Chapter 33, Verse 22.*

"The profit of the earth is for all."
—*Ecclesiastes: Chapter 5, Verse 19.*

"And ye shall hallow the fiftieth year, and proclaim liberty throughout all the land unto all the inhabitants thereof; it shall be a jubilee unto you; and ye shall return every man unto his possession, and ye shall return every man unto his family." —*Leviticus: Chapter 25, Verse 10.*

"At the end of every seven years thou shalt make a release . . . Every creditor that lendeth ought unto his neighbor shall release it; he shall not exact it of his brother, because it is called the Lord's release."
—*Deuteronomy: Chapter 15, Verses 1 and 2.*

"Wherefore ye shall do my statutes and keep my judgments and do them; and ye shall dwell in the land in safety; and the land shall yield her fruit, and ye shall eat your fill and dwell therein in safety."
—*Leviticus: Chapter 25, Verses 18 and 19.*

"Go to now, ye rich men, weep and howl for your miseries that shall come upon you.

"Your riches are corrupted, and your garments are motheaten.

"Your gold and silver is cankered; and the rust of them shall be a witness against you, and shall eat your flesh as it were fire."
—*Book of James, in the New Testament,*
Chapter 5, first verses.

"If ye walk in my statutes * * * ye shall eat your bread to the full and dwell in your land safely, and I will give peace in the land and ye shall lie there and nothing should make you afraid.

"And if ye despise my statutes * * * break my covenants * * * I will even appoint over you terror, consumption, the burning ague * * * and cause sorrow of heart." —*Leviticus, Chapter* 26, *Verses* 3 *to* 17.

"Who gave Israel for a spoil and Israel to the robbers? Did not the Lord * * * for they would not walk in His ways; neither were they obedient to his laws?"
—*Isaiah, Chapter* 42, *Verse* 24.

"Did not Moses give you the law and yet none of you keepeth the law?"
—*St. John, Chapter* 7, *Verse* 19.

And thus, today, America ignores God's law; it allows all wealth and income to the hands of the few and the millions starve in the midst of plenty.

The foundation upon which this government rests is the guarantee to humanity in the Declaration of Independence. It says:

"We hold these truths to be self evident, that all men are created equal, that they are endowed by their Creator with certain inalienable rights, that among these are Life, Liberty and the pursuit of Happiness. That to secure **these rights** (of life, liberty and happiness), governments are instituted among men, deriving their power from the consent of the governed. That whenever any form of government becomes destructive of **these ends** (of life, liberty and happiness), it is the right of the people to alter or to abolish it; and to institute new government, laying its foundation on such **principles** and organizing its power in such form, as to them shall seem **most** likely to effect their safety and **happiness.**"

JOSEPHUS:

"By these examples any one may learn how many and how great instances of wickedness men will venture upon for the sake of getting money and authority, and that they may not fail of either of them; for as when they are desirous of obtaining the same, they acquire them by ten

19

thousand evil practices; so when they are afraid of losing them, they get them confirmed to them by practices much worse than the former, as if (no) other calamity so terrible could befall them as the failure of acquiring so exalted an authority; and when they have acquired it, and by long custom found the sweetness of it, the losing it again; and since this last would be the heaviest of all afflictions, they all of them contrive and venture upon the most difficult actions, out of the fear of losing the same. But let it suffice that I have made these short reflections upon that subject."

DANIEL WEBSTER:

"I believe that the Bible is to be believed and understood in the plain and obvious meaning of its passages; for I cannot persuade myself that a book intended for the instruction and conversion of the whole world should cover its true meaning in any such mystery and doubt that none but critics and philosophers can discover it. If we abide by the principles taught in the Bible, our country will go on prospering and to prosper, but if we and our posterity neglect its instruction and its authority, no man can tell how sudden a catastrophe may overwhelm us and bury all our glory in profound obscurity."

(Page 62 of Gambrell's Baptists and Their Business)

PLATO:

"The citizen (of this ideal republic) must indeed be happy and good, and the legislator will seek to make him so; but very rich and very good at the same time he cannot be, not at least, in the sense in which the many speak of riches. For they describe by the term 'rich' the few who have the most valuable possessions, even though the owner be a rogue. . . . And good in high degree and rich in high degree at the same time, he cannot be. . . .

"The form of law which I propose would be as follows: In a state which is desirous of being saved from the greatest of all plagues—not faction, but rather distraction—there should exist among the citizens neither extreme poverty nor, again, excessive wealth, for both are productive of great evils.

"Now the legislator should determine what is to be the limit of poverty or of wealth."

20

THEOGNIS:

> "Fulness (plenty) hath ere now destroyed far more men, look you, than famine, to wit, as many as were desirous of having more than their share."

═══════════

Report of the
United States Commission on Industrial Relations
Senate Document No. 415, 64th Congress
(1916) under Woodrow Wilson's
appointment.

✦ ✦

(Extracted)

The sources from which industrial unrest springs are, when stated in full detail, almost numberless. But, upon careful analysis of their real character, they will be found to group themselves almost without exception under four main sources which include all the others. These four are:

1. Unjust distribution of wealth and income.

(Page 265)

The final control of American industry rests, therefore, in the hands of a small number of wealthy and powerful financiers.

The concentration of ownership and control is greatest in the basic industries upon which the welfare of the country must finally rest.

With few exceptions each of the great basic industries is dominated by a single large corporation, and where this is not true the control of the industry through stock ownership in supposedly independent corporations and through credit is almost, if not quite, as potent.

In such corporations, in spite of the large number of stockholders, the control through actual stock ownership rests with a very small number of persons. For example, in the United States Steel Corporation, which had in 1911 approximately 100,000 shareholders, 1.5 per cent of the stockholders held 57 per cent of the stock, while the final control rested with a single private banking house.

(Page 80)

HOW CONCENTRATION OF WEALTH HAS GONE

FROM WORSE TO RUINOUS

+ +

1916

The U. S. Industrial Relations Commision said:

"The rich, 2% of the people, own 60% of the wealth; the middle class, 33% of the people, own 35% of the wealth. The poor, 65% of the people, own 5% of the wealth. This means in brief that a little less than 2,000,000 people, who would make up a city smaller than Chicago, own 20% more of the nation's wealth than all the other 90,000,000.

1930

The Federal Trade Commission said:

"The foregoing table shows that about 1% of the estimated number of decedents owned about 59% of the estimated wealth, and that more than 90% was owned by about 13% of this number."

1934

On March 8th, 1934, a survey of the State of Ohio, as reported in the Columbus Dispatch said:

"An insight into the distribution of wealth in Ohio was given Thursday in results of a survey conducted by the research division of the special joint taxation commission. "The report made the startling observation that:

"Seventy-five per cent of all productive income is held by 5 per cent of the people, and that 10 per cent of the taxpayers hold 83 per cent of the income, while less than 2 per cent hold more than 60 per cent of all unearned income."

On September 23, 1916, in an editorial, the Saturday Evening Post said:

"The man who studies wealth in the United States from statistics only will get nowhere with the subject because all the statistics afford only an inconclusive suggestion.

"Along one statistical line you can figure out a nation bustling with wealth; along another a bloated plutocracy comprising 1% of the population lording it over a starveling horde with only a thin margin of merely well to do in between."

Again, in the year 1919, the Saturday Evening Post said:

"We want big rewards for men who do big constructive things, and jail sentences for the big fellows who steal the fruits of their work and savings of small investors.

"There have been altogether too many mavericks loose on the range, sucking cows on which they have no claim.

"There would be no real railroad mess, no necessity for trying to pare down wages in basic industries, if there had been no banker control and no flagrant watering of the stocks of these corporations."

"Yet more menacing was the concentration of power proceeding in the banking world, which even the conservative capitalistic Wall Street Journal described in 1903 as 'not merely a normal growth, but concentration that comes from combination, consolidation, and other methods employed to secure monopolistic power.' Not only this, but this concentration has not been along the lines of commercial banking. The great banks of concentration are in close alliance with financial interests intimately connected with promotion of immense enterprises, many of them being largely speculative."

On December 29th, 1820, in a speech delivered at Plymouth, on the commemoration of the first settlement of New England, Daniel Webster, the greatest American orator and statesman that ever lived, said this:

"The freest government, if it could exist, would not be long acceptable if the tendencies of the law were to create a rapid accumulation of property in few hands and to render the great mass of the population dependent and

23

penniless. In such a case the popular power would be likely to break in upon the right of property, or else the influence of property to limit and control the exercise of popular power. Universal suffrage, for example, could not long exist in a community where there was a great inequality of property.

"The holders of estates would be obliged in such case either in some way to restrain the right of suffrage, or else such right of suffrage would soon divide the property. In the nature of things, those who have not property, and see their neighbors possess much more than they think them to need, can not be favorable to laws made for the protection of property. When this class becomes numerous it grows clamorous. It looks on property as its prey and plunder, and is naturally ready, at all times, for violence and revolution."

I quote from the Reverend Harry Emerson Fosdick, Pastor of the Baptist Church of which John D. Rockefeller, Sr. and Jr., are members, from a speech on December 28, 1930:

"See the picture of the world today—communism rising as a prodigious world power and all the capitalistic nations arming themselves to the teeth to fly at each other's throats and tear each other to pieces . . . Capitalism is on trial . . . Our whole capitalistic society is on trial.

"First, within itself, for obviously there is something the matter with the operation of a system that over the western world leaves millions and millions of people out of work who want work, and millions more in the sinister shadow of poverty.

"Second, capitalism is on trial with communism for its world competitor.

"The verbal damning of communism now prevalently popular in the United States will get us nowhere. The decision between capitalism and communism hinges on one point: Can capitalism adjust itself to the new age?"

FRANKLIN D. ROOSEVELT, at Chesterton, Maryland, on October 21, 1933, as reported by the Associated Press said:

"As I recall the words of a professor in my school, the wider a distribution of wealth there is in the proper way, the more we can make it possible for the men and

24

women of the land to have the necessities of life in such shape that they will not have to lie awake at night worrying where the food tomorrow will come from. Then, and only then, will we have the security necessary for the country."

The immortal Abraham Lincoln said:

"Inasmuch as most good things are produced by labor, it follows that all such things of right belong to those whose labor has produced them. But it has so happened in all ages of the world that some have labored and others have without labor enjoyed a large proportion of the fruits. This is wrong and should not continue. To secure to each laborer the whole product of his labor, or as nearly as possible, is a worthy subject of any good Government."

President Theodore Roosevelt said in one of his public addresses:

"I feel that we shall ultimately have to consider the adoption of some such scheme as that of a progressive tax on all fortunes beyond a certain amount, either given in life or devised or bequeathed upon death to any individual—a tax so framed as to put it out of the power of the owner of one of these enormous fortunes to hand down more than a certain amount to any one individual."

St. Louis Post-Dispatch of May 27, 1931:

Senator James Couzens (Michigan) does not believe the depression in this country is due to world depression.

Nor does he believe that our recovery depends upon world recovery.

He believes, and emphatically says, that American capitalists caused the American depression mainly by taking an exorbitant share of the earnings of American industry, and that recovery can be accomplished only by securing the livelihoods and increasing the purchasing power of American workers.

In his Madison Square Garden speech even our last President, Mr. Hoover, said:

"My conception of America is a land where men and women may walk in ordered liberty, where they may enjoy the advantages of wealth, not concentrated in the hands of a few but diffused through the lives of all."

25

In the address by President Hoover delivered at Indianapolis, here is what he said:

> Above all schemes of public works which have no reproductive value would result in sheer waste. Public works would result in sheer waste.
>
> The remedy to economic depression is not waste but the creation and distribution of wealth.

Here is a quotation from the dean of the Harvard Graduate School of Business Administration, Wallace B. Donham:

> If we have not in our several countries the brains, ability, and the cooperative spirit necessary to cure such world-wide conditions as those in which we now find ourselves, then our mass production, our scientific progress, our control over nature may actually destroy civilization.

It was hundred of years ago when Lord Bacon sounded his warning that there would be starvation in the land of the plenty, unless the wealth be spread among all of the people. Said he:

> "Concerning the materials of sedition, it is a thing well to be considered—for the surest way to prevent seditions (if the times to bear it), is to take away the matter of them."

In other words, if you want to avoid revolutions, take away the cause of revolutions. To quote further:

> "For if there be fuel prepared, it is hard to tell whence the spark shall come that shall set it on fire. The matter of sedition is of two kinds, much poverty and much discontentment. It is certain, so many overthrown estates, so many votes for trouble . . . This same 'multis utile bellum' is an assured and infallible sign of a State disposed to seditions and troubles; and if this poverty and broken estate in the better sort be joined with a want and necessity in the mean people, the danger is imminent and great —for the rebellions of the belly are the worst.
>
> "Above all things, good policy is to be used, that the treasures and monies in a State be not gathered into few hands, for otherwise, a State may have a great stock, and the people starve."

From the encyclical of Pope Pius XI, dated May 18, 1932:

> "From greed arises mutual distrust that casts a blight on all human dealings; from greed arises hateful envy which makes a man consider the advantages of another as losses to himself; from greed arises narrow individualism which orders and subordinates everything to its own advantage without taking account of others, on the contrary, cruelly trampling under foot all rights of others. Hence the disorder and inequality from which arises the accumulation of the wealth of nations in the hands of a small group of individuals who manipulate the market of the world at their own caprice, to the immense harm of the masses, as we showed last year in our encyclical letter, "Quadragesimo Anno.""

WEALTH INCREASES FOR FEW, WHILE WAGES DECREASE

Rev. Charles E. Coughlin, in a sermon which he delivered Sunday, November 27, 1932, says:

"The wealth being produced by agriculture and industry was being siphoned off and retained by a comparative few.

Although the true function of the machine is to spread leisure and opportunity for mental and spiritual development, its use has been increasingly perverted. Not only has there been a steady arithmetical increase in unemployment; it has been accompanied by a steady increase of wealth in the hands of the few. The wealth created by the machines has grown in appalling disproportion to the owners of machines.

In 1922 the total dividends paid by all corporations in the United States was $930,648,000. In 1929 the dividends paid were $3,478,000,000, an increase of 356 per cent.

Here, then, we have the third characteristic which is best expressed by the phrase: "Concentration of wealth in the hands of a few." The development of mass production is being accompanied by the destruction of mass consumption and mass purchasing power.

It is hoped that the efficient laws of yesterday which permitted this unjust concentration of wealth and this unreasonable share of profits to fall into the hands of a few shall not be permitted to exist beyond the life of the next presidential term.

Just as we have been taught to look with disdain and contempt upon physical slavery, so future generations shall revert to the period which has just passed with similar feelings—an age

27

of industrial and financial slavery which is more apparent when we consider that the annual income for all people in the United States increased from $65,949,000,000 in the year 1919 to $89,419,000,000 in 1928—an increase of approximately twenty-three and one-half billion dollars, despite the fact that the total volume of wages paid was $649,000,000 less than in 1927. The greater the wealth of this Nation the less were its wages for working man and the farmer."

EXTRACT FROM REMARKS

of

HON. JAMES COUZENS

of Michigan

In The Senate of The United States

March 14, 1933

Mr. President, the National Economy League, the big-business organizations, and the chambers of commerce ought to hang their heads in shame for driving this thing through Congress. I wonder whether this Government is not a government of the money lenders rather than a government of the people. You may call that demagoguery. I know my friend the Senator from Louisiana (Mr. Long) is condemned because he makes these unhappy comparisons; but notwithstanding what you may think of him, notwithstanding the ridicule the great press of the country may heap on him, nevertheless the comparisons he makes from day to day, and which I have the honor to make to-day, are odious; and the impression on the American people will be so great that it will be years and years before any Senator who votes for this legislation will be able adequately to defend himself before the American people.

Extracted from "The Epic of America" by James Truslow Adams:

"Conditions adapted for a more or less equalitarian society, combined with the new technology, began to create an unprecedented gulf between the wage earner and the incipient billionaire. . . . The size of individual fortunes had been growing with each generation . . . in an alarming degree. * * * There seemed room for everything except the heart of man and the old independence of the individual to work out his own life and scale of values * * * (Prior to 1914) We had our minds intensely focused on moral problems and the effort to work out ways and means of making

28

our own land a better and cleaner one in all its aspects * * * The progress that was at last being made in controlling instead of destroying big business, all seemed to promise the nearer fulfillment of the American dream. Suddenly the whole of Western European civilization appeared to have burst into flames. * * *

"Statistics when used nationally can be very misleading, and although it was true that the national wealth had been enormously increased and that the country was 'prosperous,' the new wealth was very unevenly distributed. * * * In a modern industrial state an economic base is essential for all. We point with pride to our 'National income,' but the nation is only an aggregate of individual men and women, and when we turn from the single figure of total income to the incomes of individuals, we find a marked injustice in its distribution. There is no reason why wealth, which is a social product, should not be more equitably controlled and distributed in the interests of society. * * *

"A system that steadily increases the gulf between the ordinary man and the super-rich, that permits the resources of society to be gathered into personal fortunes that afford their owners millions of income a year, with only the chance that here and there a few may be moved to confer some of their surplus upon the public in ways chosen wholly by themselves, is assuredly a wasteful and unjust system. * * * Nor is it likely to be voluntarily altered by those who benefit most by it. No ruling class has ever willingly abdicated.

"The members of the Morgan and Rockefeller groups together (about 1903—it is far worse now) held 341 directorships in 112 banks, railroads, insurance and other corporations, having aggregate resources under their control of $22,245,000,000. In an after-dinner speech one of the group made the tactical mistake of declaring that it had been said that the business of the United States was then controlled by twelve men, of whom he was one, and that the statement was true. This remark, made among friends, was deleted from the printed report of the speech when given to the public, but the public was well enough aware of the general situation without such admission. Never before had such colossal power concentrated so rapidly into the hands of a few, whether we consider the resources and income at their command, the population affected by their orders and acts, or the millions of persons in their direct employ."

29

Mr. Guglielmo Marconi, inventor of the radio and the wireless, who is one of the greatest inventors in the world, on March 9, 1934, said:

"The affirmation that science and the machine are responsible for the world crisis and unemployment must be definitely rejected. They have made it possible for man, with enormously reduced effort, still to have everything he needs for a life of comfort.

"It is not the machine or science that have provoked the ills from which we suffer.

"We have been cheated of the advantages they have brought by a defective distribution of the wealth and resources Providence has given us in abundance, and above all by human selfishness."

From
"THE DOOM OF AMERICA'S DREAM"
speech of
HUEY P. LONG
In the Senate of the United States
Monday, April 4, 1932

We have passed laws, and have enacted various and sundry things, but we have never been able to create a commission that lasted very long. We have never been able to get a rule of law interpreted that stood for any particular time unless they began, by some contrivance or machination, to make the element, that was affected by it the master of the law that was being enforced. They have become the masters of the law.

How long is it going to last? How long can it last? How long will it last? I tell you, Mr. President, it can not last very long.

I am not asking any man in the United States Senate to do anything harmful to the rich people of this country. If you want to do them a favor, provide some way to put some of that wealth among some of the people of this country. If you want to make their lives secure, provide a way for relieving the anxieties of 90 per cent of the people in this country to-day who are in absolute fear of want and impoverishment. Provide a way whereby the world is going to provide a living for the people of the United States, if you love these rich people as much as I love them. Yes, sir; provide a way to distribute it. If we sit here in this Congress and let this tax bill go back with a clause ipso facto annulling the law at the end of two years, so that these taxes will no longer be collected; if we do not raise these surtaxes and these inheritance taxes to a point where they can not continue to perpetuate these massive fortunes in the United States, like a snowball going down-hill; if we do not regulate them, when you have gone and gathered it all, in what condition are you going to leave the country?

But Why Not the Dream of America?

But O Mr. President, if we could simply let the people enjoy the wealth and the accumulations and the earnings and the income and the machinery and the contrivances that we have. If, with the invention of every machine, we could secure the education of every man; if with increased production of every kind there could be less toil, more hours of pleasure and recreation; if there could be a happy and contented people enjoying what the Almighty has made it possible to provide; if there could be people clothed with the materials that we have to clothe them with to-day, and no place to put them; if the people could be fed with the food that we have to feed them with, and no place to put it; if the people could be sheltered in the homes we have to-day that the Federal Land Bank has taken away from them because they can not pay the interest on the mortgages—if that could be done, if we could distribute this surplus wealth, while leaving these rich people all the luxuries they can possibly use, what a different world this would be.

"Thy Soul Shall Be Required"

Do not take away anything they need. Leave them with every palace, with every convenience, with every comfort; but do not allow the concentration and stagnation of wealth to reach the point where it is a national calamity.

Will we do that? Will they do it? No; we know they will not do it. Will we do it for them? Maybe we will. Maybe we will not. There ought to be a coalition of the people; there ought to be a coalition of the Senators representing the rights of the people in a situation of this kind, as efficient as is the coalition of the bipartisan movement recommending and sponsoring the other side of the field.

31

We can do this. If we do not we will leave these masters of finance and fame and fortune like the man in the book of old, who said to himself, so the Bible tells us:

"I will pull down my barns, and build greater; and there will I bestow all my fruits and my goods.

"And I will say to my soul: Soul, thou hast much goods laid up for many years; take thine ease, eat, drink, and be merry.

"But God said unto him: Thou fool, this night thy soul shall be required of thee."

✦   ✦

FROM JOHN MILTON'S COMUS

If every just man that pines with want
Had but a moderate and beseeming share
Of that which lewdly pampered Luxury
Now heaps upon some few with vast excess,
Nature's full blessings would be well dispensed
In unsuperfluous even proportion
And she no whit encumbered with her store;
And then the giver would be better thanked,
His praise due paid; for swinish Gluttony
Ne'er looks to Heaven amidst his gorgeous feast
But with besotted base ingratitude
Crams, and blasphemes his feeder.

INDEX

INDEX—Continued

INDEX—Continued

COSIMO is a specialty publisher of books and publications that inspire, inform, and engage readers. Our mission is to offer unique books to niche audiences around the world.

COSIMO BOOKS publishes books and publications for innovative authors, nonprofit organizations, and businesses. **COSIMO BOOKS** specializes in bringing books back into print, publishing new books quickly and effectively, and making these publications available to readers around the world.

COSIMO CLASSICS offers a collection of distinctive titles by the great authors and thinkers throughout the ages. At **COSIMO CLASSICS** timeless works find new life as affordable books, covering a variety of subjects including: Business, Economics, History, Personal Development, Philosophy, Religion & Spirituality, and much more!

COSIMO REPORTS publishes public reports that affect your world, from global trends to the economy, and from health to geopolitics.

FOR MORE INFORMATION CONTACT US AT
INFO@COSIMOBOOKS.COM

➤ if you are a book lover interested in our current catalog of books

➤ if you represent a bookstore, book club, or anyone else interested in special discounts for bulk purchases

➤ if you are an author who wants to get published

➤ if you represent an organization or business seeking to publish books and other publications for your members, donors, or customers.

**COSIMO BOOKS ARE ALWAYS
AVAILABLE AT ONLINE BOOKSTORES**

VISIT COSIMOBOOKS.COM
BE INSPIRED, BE INFORMED